Donkeys

James Maclaine

Illustrated by Jeremy Norton

Additional illustrations by Roger Simó
Designed by Amy Manning and Sam Whibley

Donkey consultant: Professor David Macdonald CBE,
Wildlife Conservation Research Unit, Zoology Department, University of Oxford
Reading consultant: Alison Kelly

Contents

Head to hoof

All donkeys have large heads and big ears.

They have long tails with hairy tips.

They have hard hooves too.

Helpful donkeys

In some parts of the world people use donkeys to help with work because they're small and strong.

Donkeys can carry heavy things on their backs for long distances.

They are good at pulling carts and tools on farms.

Donkeys can also guard sheep or goats against wild dogs.

This donkey
lives on a farm
with a horse.

People often keep donkeys with horses.
Donkeys help horses to stay calm.

5

In the wild

Donkeys live in the wild too.

These donkeys are called African wild asses.
They live in deserts and on dry grasslands.

African wild asses are rare. There are only
a few hundred of them left in the world.

Most donkeys in the wild were released by people or escaped from farms. They are known as feral donkeys.

These feral donkeys live in Cyprus.

Feral donkeys on the Italian island of Asinara are white and have pink noses.

Hairy coats

A donkey's body is covered in pale or dark hair. This is called its coat.

Donkeys grow extra hair in winter to make their coats thick and warm.

They lose this hair when it's summer. The hair falls out in clumps.

Most donkeys have a cross-shaped pattern on their shoulders.

A donkey has a mane of long, dark hair on its head and neck.

Keeping clean

Donkeys try to keep their coats healthy and clean. They remove dirt and tangled hair using their teeth.

These donkeys live together. They're nibbling each other's coats clean.

This donkey is rolling on dusty ground.

This helps it to rub off any insects that make its skin itch.

Donkeys also roll in dust to dry their coats when they're sweaty.

Greedy grazers

Donkeys spend more than half the day eating. They have strong, rough teeth that are good for chewing.

This donkey is grazing on grass.

Donkeys also eat leaves and
seeds on bushes and trees.

Sometimes they
chew bark from
tree trunks too.

Donkeys on farms
are given hay and
grain to eat.

Small sips

Donkeys drink small amounts of water. They only need to drink every two to three days.

People who keep donkeys give them water in large containers.

In the wild, donkeys find watering holes or rivers when they want to drink.

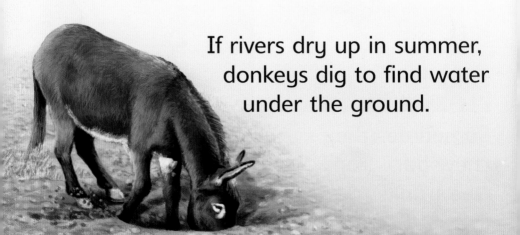

If rivers dry up in summer, donkeys dig to find water under the ground.

Some donkeys live in places where it is very cold in winter. They get water by eating snow.

Male donkeys

In the wild, an adult male donkey often lives with a group of females. He tries to keep other males away from them.

A male donkey leaves his dung around the area where he lives.

When another male sniffs the dung, he finds out that a male already lives here.

If the two male donkeys meet, one may try to chase the other away.

Sometimes male donkeys fight to see who is strongest.

These donkeys are trying to kick and bite each other.

Baby donkeys

Baby donkeys are called foals. A mother donkey carries her baby inside her for about a year.

When a mother is ready to have her foal, she starts to roll on her back.

She then lies on her side. Soon her foal is born.

A mother sniffs her newborn foal and licks its body clean and dry.

This foal was born
less than an hour ago.

It can already stand up but its legs
are very wobbly.

Growing up

A foal stays close to its mother as it grows up. It spends lots of time drinking her milk.

This young foal is sucking milk from one of the two teats on its mother's tummy.

Foals grow up very quickly.

They learn how to run when they're just one day old.

They start to eat grass a week after they're born.

A foal drinks milk until it's nine months old. It folds down its ears to ask its mother for milk.

Staying safe

Donkeys have several ways of keeping themselves safe.

Some wild donkeys live in groups. This makes it hard for animals to attack them.

Donkeys usually run away if they're scared of something. They can run fast.

A donkey kicks its front hooves to scare away an animal attacking it.

Donkeys also keep themselves safe
from the Sun, so they
don't get too hot.

These donkeys have found a place in
the shade to rest.

Noisy donkeys

Donkeys often make hee-haw noises. This is called braying.

This donkey is breathing in and out very fast to bray.

A female donkey swishes her tail and brays if she wants to attract a male.

Male donkeys sometimes growl at each other while they're fighting.

Donkeys in the wild make noises to tell each other where they are.

A donkey can turn and bend its ears to hear sounds better.

Donkey signs

When donkeys want to show how they feel, they make faces and move their bodies in different ways.

A donkey folds back its ears and shows its teeth if it is scared.

Sometimes when donkeys become angry they kick out their back legs.

Donkeys prick up their ears and sniff each other's snouts to greet each other.

This donkey is resting its head on another donkey's neck.

Donkeys only do this when they like one another.

Caring for donkeys

People who keep donkeys have to give them things to take good care of them.

Donkeys need a large, grassy field where they can run and graze.

Their coats aren't waterproof, so they need a place to shelter when it rains.

If it gets very cold, donkeys need a warm stable to stay in.

This donkey is
licking a block
of salt.

Donkeys have
to eat salt to stay healthy.

Glossary

Here are some of the words in this book you might not know. This page tells you what they mean.

 hoof - the hard part at the end of a donkey's foot.

 feral - an animal that was once kept by people but now lives in the wild.

 mane - the long hair that grows on a donkey's head and down its neck.

 graze - to eat grass. Donkeys spend lots of time grazing.

 foal - a baby donkey. A mother donkey has one foal at a time.

 teat - part of a mother donkey's body where milk comes out.

 bray - a hee-haw sound that donkeys often make.

Websites to visit

You can visit exciting websites to find out more about donkeys. For links to sites with video clips and activities, go to the Usborne Quicklinks website at **www.usborne.com/quicklinks** and type in the keywords "**beginners donkeys**".

Always ask an adult before using the internet and make sure you follow these basic rules:
1. Never give out personal information, such as your name, address, school or telephone number.
2. If a website asks you to type in your name or email address, check with an adult first.

The websites are regularly reviewed and the links at Usborne Quicklinks are updated. However, Usborne Publishing is not responsible and does not accept liability for the content or availability of any website other than its own. We recommend that children are supervised while on the internet.

Donkeys tilt back their heads and curl up their lips when they want to smell or taste something in the air.

Index

Acknowledgements

Photographic manipulation by John Russell

Photo credits

The publishers are grateful to the following for permission to reproduce material:
Cover © Klein & Hubert/naturepl.com; **p1** © Juniors/Juniors/SuperStock; **p2-3** © Klein & Hubert/naturepl.
com; **p5** © Juniors/Juniors/SuperStock; **p6** © Biosphoto/Biosphoto/SuperStock; **p7** © Robin Weaver/Alamy
Stock Photo; **p8-9** © leekriss/Thinkstock; **p10** © Bildagentur Geduldig/Alamy Stock Photo; **p11** © Harald
Lange/ullstein bild/Getty Images; **p12** © vilainecrevette/Thinkstock; **p13** © J.-L. Klein and M.-L. Hubert/FLPA;
p15 © J.-L. Klein and M.-L. Hubert/FLPA; **p16-17** © Marka/Marka/SuperStock; **p19** © J.-L. Klein and M.-L.
Hubert/FLPA; **p20** © David & Micha Sheldon/Masterfile/Corbis; **p23** © Biosphoto/Biosphoto/SuperStock;
p24 © Rosemary Calvert/Getty Images; **p27** © Hemis.fr/Hemis.fr/SuperStock;
p29 © Donkey Welfare with Heart; **p31** © Rachele Totaro/Getty Images

Every effort has been made to trace and acknowledge ownership of copyright. If any rights have
been omitted, the publishers offer to rectify this in any subsequent editions following notification.

Sun, moon and stars

Farm animals

Elizabeth I

Rubbish & Recycling

Dogs

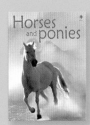
Horses and ponies

Spiders

Planes

Cats

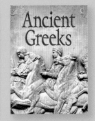
Ancient Greeks

VOLCANOES

Dinosaurs

Your Body

Armour

Sharks

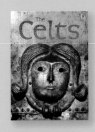
The Celts

VIKINGS

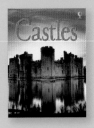
Castles

How flowers grow

Digging up the past

Living in space

Caterpillars and Butterflies

Ballet

Pirates

EGYPTIANS

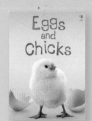
Eggs and Chicks

ROMANS

Weather

Tadpoles and frogs

Why do we eat?

Under the sea

Bears

AZTECS

TRUCKS

Night Animals

Firefighters

Antarctica

Bugs

COWBOYS

Planet Earth

London

Seashore

China

Dangerous Animals

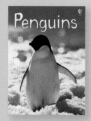
Rainforests

Trees

Reptiles

Ships

Bats

Penguins

Contents

CHAPTER ONE

Amara ran down the path to the gate that led to the meadow, the early morning dew soaking into her trainers. There had been a storm in the night, and branches lay scattered across the grassy track, but the wind had faded now and everything felt fresh and bright.

Reaching the gate, Amara's gaze flew to the eight beautiful ponies who were grazing at the far end of the meadow – one grey, one palomino, one bay-and-white, two chestnuts, another bay, one grey-and-white and one sleek black with a glossy mane.

"Ember!" she called.

The coal-black pony lifted his head. A whinny burst from him and Amara felt fireworks of happiness exploding inside her as he cantered to meet her, his coat gleaming in the rays of the April sun. She didn't even stop to open the gate but scrambled over it to get to him.

Ember skidded to a halt and gently thrust his head against her chest. Amara wrapped her arms around his neck, resting her forehead against his and breathing in his sweet smell.

You're here very early, Amara. Ember's mouth didn't move but she could hear his

thoughts as clearly as if he had spoken aloud.

*The wind woke me up in the night. I
couldn't get back to sleep so I thought I'd
come and see you.* She loved living just down
the lane from the stables. It made visiting
Ember very easy! *Let's do some magic before
everyone else gets here.*

Ember snorted in delight. Like all the
horses in the meadow, he was an elemental

horse – a horse with magical powers. His
power was fire, while the others could do
things like make plants grow, make it rain or
conjure sandstorms. There were elemental
horses all over the world. They chose boys or
girls to be their True Riders, someone who
could help them learn how to control their
magic, then worked together to do good.

Let's do some magic now! Ember said.

A thrill ran through Amara as Ember
cantered away, reared up and transformed
from a beautiful pony into a majestic horse.
His soft mane and tail changed into red and
orange flames and his eyes glowed with
golden fire. She loved seeing him in his
magical elemental form! Running over to
him, she grabbed his fiery mane and vaulted
on to his back. The magic flames tickled her

skin but didn't burn her. She dug her knees into his sides. "Gallop, Ember!" she cried.

Ember raced away around the meadow. Amara shouted out loud with excitement. Only a few weeks ago, she had been scared to ride Ember without a saddle but now she trusted him and she loved the moments when she was able to gallop on him while he was in his true form. Her long brown plaits flew out behind her and she felt her body tingle with the magic that was flowing through him.

Skidding to a halt near a fallen branch which had split from an oak tree in the night, Ember stamped his front hooves. A ball of fire flew at the bough and as it hit it, the wood burst into flames. The fire blazed up, reaching towards the blue sky. The ponies grazing at the other end of the meadow raised their heads to watch.

Hold on tight, Ember told her.

Amara grabbed his mane as he galloped forward and jumped high over the branch before turning and stamping his hooves again, controlling the flames and making them shrink smaller and smaller until they flickered and went out, leaving just a cloud of grey smoke floating in the air.

The other ponies whinnied with excitement. It was very difficult to control an element as strong as fire.

"That was brilliant, Ember!" Amara cried.

Ember changed back into his pony form. He was panting slightly – doing magic used a lot of energy – but Amara could feel happiness coursing through him. *You're so*

much better at controlling your magic now than you used to be, she told him.

He turned his head to nuzzle her leg. *That's because I've got you to help me.*

She patted his neck. *I don't really do anything.*

You believe in me and trust me; that makes all the difference.

Leaning forward, Amara put her arms round his neck and buried her face in his silky mane. She was so lucky he'd chosen her to be his True Rider!

She hugged him for a long moment and then dismounted. *I'd better see if Jill needs any help clearing up after the storm,* she told him. Moonlight Stables, where Ember and the other elemental horses in the meadow lived, was owned by Jill Reed. Jill had been a True Rider when she was younger but her horse, Shula, a fire horse like Ember, had died in a dreadful accident. Jill had made it her life's work to try and help other elemental horses find their True Riders. Not all of the horses and ponies at Moonlight Stables were magical though. Jill's own horse, Apollo, was a retired racehorse and the riding school ponies were just regular ponies.

The wind was blowing really hard last night, wasn't it? Ember said as they walked to the gate. He glanced back at his friends. *Sirocco tried to use his wind magic to control it but the storm was too strong. He can't control the wind when it turns into a storm like that. He has no control over the rain and thunder.*

I'm glad it's stopped now, said Amara. *I want today to be perfect – it's Kalini's first proper day here.*

Kalini's your friend from school, isn't she? Ember said.

Amara nodded. She and Kalini sat together in class. Amara had only lived in Eastwall and been going to St Mary's Primary School for a few months but she and Kalini had quickly become good friends. It helped that they both loved ponies!

Kalini hadn't had many proper riding lessons but she knew lots about horses because she loved to read books about them. When Amara had told her that Jill ran a riding club at the stables where boys and girls could work on the yard in exchange for lessons, Kalini had begged her parents to join. She'd had a trial session the weekend before but today was her first proper day helping out at the stables, and to celebrate, they were going to have a sleepover at Amara's house that night.

Forest and Sparks still haven't chosen their True Riders, said Ember, looking at a slim dark brown pony and a stockier bay-and-white pony. *Maybe one of them will choose Kalini.*

That would be amazing! Amara said.

She had been longing to tell Kalini about the elemental horses but Jill had told her that the only people who could know the elemental horses' secret were True Riders or Legacy Riders, whose parents or grandparents had been True Riders.

Reaching the gate, Amara gave Ember a

last hug. "I'll be back to see you soon," she promised. Climbing the gate, she set off up the path to the yard. Ember whinnied as she left and, looking back, Amara saw the love in his eyes and felt her heart sing. There was nothing better than being a True Rider. She really hoped Kalini would get a chance to discover that too!

CHAPTER TWO

Amara hurried past the elemental horses'
stable block – the Meadow Stables. It was in
a quiet section of the yard at the top of the
path that led to the meadow. She passed the
hay barn, breathing in the sweet scent, and
went on to the main stables where the non-
magical horses and ponies were kept. Each
stable door was painted a different pastel
colour. The yard was usually quite tidy,
however the storm in the night had caused

havoc. The mucking out tools had blown off their racks, the wheelbarrows were lying on their sides and piles of straw had blown on to the yard. Jill was sweeping up. She was in her fifties with blonde hair and skin that was tanned from being outsideall day.

"Morning!" she called, seeing Amara. "That was a rainy night, wasn't it?"

"It really was," Amara agreed, starting to put the mucking out tools back in the rack. "Are all the ponies OK?"

"Yes, I checked them as soon as I got up," said Jill. "I thought I'd leave them out in their fields while I tidied up. We've got a busy day ahead. There are lessons all morning and then I want to have an extra-long training session this afternoon. It's only a week until the competition."

Jill ran a mounted games squad that competed in a local league against teams from other riding schools. In mounted games competitions, teams of four or five riders took part in a number of different races, winning points depending on where their team placed in each race. At the end, the team with the most points was declared the winner. The races were very fast and the riders had to be able to vault on and off their horses, pick up objects from the ground and pass them to other riders at a gallop. All whilst racing as quickly as they could around poles. The riders could only compete in the local league while they were under fifteen years old. The ponies in the Moonlight Stables squad were all elemental horses but when they competed they stayed in their pony form and never used their powers.

Amara wasn't nearly as experienced a rider as the other members of the squad, but Bea, one of the normal team riders, couldn't compete at the weekend because she was going to be a bridesmaid at her cousin's wedding, and so Amara was going to take her place. She was really looking forward to it, although she felt quite anxious whenever Jill mentioned how close the competition was. She didn't want to let the team down.

Amara suddenly had an idea. "Jill, do you think Kalini could start riding in the squad? She could ride Forest or Sparks."

To her disappointment, Jill shook her head. "I only put people into the squad when I believe they have potential to be a True Rider – or when a pony chooses them, like

Ember chose you." She seemed to see the disappointment on Amara's face. "It may happen one day but I need to get to know Kalini first." Hearing a car in the lane, she glanced round. "Ah, excellent, it's Imogen and Alex."

Imogen Fairfax and Alex Brahler were in Amara's class at school and lived near each other on the other side of town. They were both members of the Moonlight Stables riding club as well as being True Riders. Imogen had been chosen by Tide, a slim, snow-white pony who could control water, and Alex had been chosen by Rose, a chestnut pony with a flaxen mane and tail, who could make plants grow. They were both in the mounted games team.

They waved to Jill and Amara and jogged

up the yard, Imogen's pigtails bouncing on her shoulders. "Morning, you two!" called Jill. "Good to see you so bright and early. Can you help Amara tidy up here while I start bringing ponies in?"

"Sure," said Imogen, straightening her glasses on her nose.

"How come it's so messy today?" said Alex,

grabbing a yard brush and starting to sweep enthusiastically beside Amara as Jill hurried off. He always did everything with loads of energy.

"It was the storm in the night," said Amara.

"What storm?" said Imogen.

"The big storm," said Amara. She saw their puzzled faces. "Didn't you two hear the thunder?"

"There wasn't any by my house," said Alex.

"Or mine," Imogen added.

"Seriously?" said Amara. "It was really strong here."

"Weird," said Imogen. "Are the ponies all OK?"

Amara nodded. "I went to the meadow first thing. They're all fine."

"Phew!" Alex pushed his brush into the

pile of swept-up straw so hard that it all flew up into the air, covering Imogen.

"Alex!" she laughed, taking her glasses off and cleaning them.

"Oops, sorry, Immy," he apologised.

"That's OK. At least it wasn't the dirty straw. Maybe you should pick the wheelbarrows up and put them away while I sweep," she suggested.

As they tidied up, they talked about the games competition. "It's brilliant you're on the team for this competition," Imogen said to Amara.

Amara smiled happily. When she'd first joined the yard, she'd felt left out because she had sensed Alex and Imogen were hiding something from her, but after Ember had chosen Amara to be his True Rider, Imogen

24

and Alex didn't have to keep the magic secret from her any more and they'd all become friends.

"Yeah, you'll have to take part in mine and Immy's tradition," said Alex. "After every competition, we go to Marco's Ice Cream Parlour on the High Street. They do the best ice cream sundaes!"

"And banana splits," said Imogen. "You'll join us, won't you?"

"Definitely," said Amara in delight. She hadn't been to Marco's yet but she'd walked past it a few times and really wanted to visit it.

"Should we go to the meadow this evening when everyone's gone and do some magic?" said Alex eagerly.

"I can't," said Amara. "Kalini's starting

here today and she's staying at my house after. I wish I could though," she added, remembering how Ember had set fire to the branch and jumped over it. "I want to show you what Ember did earlier! He—"

"Ssh!" Imogen said quickly, motioning behind her. Kalini had just arrived and was walking up the yard towards them.

Amara quickly stopped talking. Kalini's long dark hair was tied back in a ponytail with two glittery pink slides that matched her pink coat.

"Hi!" Kalini called, giving Alex and Imogen a slightly shy look. Although they were all in the same year at school, Alex and Imogen hung round with the popular group.

"Hi," they said, giving her friendly smiles.

Alex turned to Imogen. "Now we've tidied

up, should we go to the meadow and see the ponies?"

Imogen nodded. "OK. See you later, Kalini."

They went off together. Kalini smiled and looked around. "This is so cool," she said to Amara, her hazel eyes shining. "I can't believe I'm actually going to be helping here."

"It's great, isn't it?" said Amara, linking arms with her. "Come on, I'll show you where to put your things and then we can

find Jill and tell her you're here."

Excitement fizzed inside her at the thought of spending a day at Moonlight Stables with Kalini. Ponies and her best friend – what could be better than that?

CHAPTER THREE

The morning flew by. The riding school
ponies needed grooming, and there were
water buckets to fill and stables to sweep
out. Then the first group of children arrived
for their lesson and Amara, Kalini, Alex and
Imogen had to lead the ponies while Jill
instructed the riders. After that, they had to
brush the ponies down and put up jumps for
the more experienced riders.

At lunchtime, they took their packed

lunches out to the riding arena – and sat on a pile of jumps near the gate. Amara had a feeling Kalini was still feeling a bit shy with the others because she didn't chat as much as she usually did. *Hopefully she'll relax with them soon,* she thought.

When he had finished eating, Alex jumped to his feet. "Let's have an obstacle race before we get the ponies ready for games training."

Imogen groaned. "Can't we just sit here for a while?"

"Sitting's boring," said Alex, jogging on the spot. "OK, you lazy lot stay there and I'll put the course out." The girls watched him as he dashed around, pulling jumps and poles into place and unrolling a tarpaulin sheet.

He ran back over, holding a cone. "You start by jumping the red-and-white jump, then crawl under the tarpaulin, throw a beanbag into the bucket, jump the green jump, then go out through the far gate and get back here the quickest way you can. When you touch this cone, the timer stops. Fastest one to get back is the winner! Bet that's me!"

Amara folded her arms. "We'll see about that!"

"Accept it, Amara," Alex said airily. "I'm the best."

"Yeah, the best at boasting!" Imogen said with a grin. "OK, I'll go first!"

Imogen was a quick runner but she took her time crawling under the tarpaulin. "There are bugs under here, Alex!" she shrieked. "Ew!" When she got to the next jump, she looked about to jump over it but then tripped and stopped. "Whoops, first refusal!" she said. She jumped it the second time but then when she came through the gate it took her ages to get back to the cone because of the thick undergrowth that grew beside the fence. She fell over twice.

"OK, I'm officially rubbish!" she said, laughing as she climbed back over the fence and touched the cone.

Amara went next. She was determined to get a fast time but she missed the bucket with the beanbags three times and struggled through the bracken and brambles at the end.

"Not bad," said Alex, looking at the stopwatch. "But now it's time for you all to watch the expert!" He raced around the course but he chucked the beanbags so hard that he missed the bucket several times like

Amara had. Running through the gate, he climbed up on to the top of fence and began to walk along it like a tightrope walker, avoiding the brambles that had slowed both Imogen and Amara down.

"That's cheating!" exclaimed Amara.

"No it's not. I just said you had to get back here as quickly as you can," said Alex, grinning. "I told you I'm the best— whoa!" he yelled as he lost his balance and landed in a patch of bracken.

The girls burst out laughing.

"You're the best, are you, Alex?" Imogen called.

Pulling a face at her, Alex threw himself over the fence and slammed his hand down on the cone. "Stop the clock! What was my time? Am I the winner?"

"You're the fastest so far but Kalini's still got to go," Amara replied.

"Go for it, Kalini!" Imogen encouraged.

Kalini set off. Amara was surprised to see how fast she could run. She'd never really seen Kalini sprint at school, but she raced over the ground. She cleared the first jump and wriggled under the tarpaulin before reaching the beanbags, where she paused for a moment, weighing up the distance she had to throw them.

"Too much hesitation. She's never going to beat my time," said Alex confidently.

But Kalini got the beanbag into the bucket first time and then she was off again, running like a hare. When she reached the gate, to everyone's surprise she turned to the right instead of the left.

"What are you doing? That's the long way round!" shouted Alex.

"I know, but it's also the easiest," Kalini called back.

Amara realised she was right. There was far less undergrowth the way Kalini had chosen to go. She raced around the outside of the school, climbed over the fence and touched the cone.

"Well?" Amara said to Imogen, who had the stopwatch and was timing Kalini.

A smile spread across Imogen's face. "Kalini's the winner!"

Amara whooped and Imogen clapped.

Alex put his hands on his hips. "That's so not fair!" he said in mock disgust.

Kalini shot him a slightly shy, teasing grin. "I guess it looks like I'm the best."

Alex grinned back. "OK, you are. Well done. You're really fast."

"And good at throwing," said Imogen. "I bet Jill will ask you to try out for the mounted games squad when you've been coming here a bit longer."

Amara felt a thrill of delight. *I'll do everything I can to make it happen,* she promised herself.

"Amara! Concentrate!" Jill's voice snapped as Amara missed the stick Alex was holding out for her to take and it clattered to the floor.

"Sorry!" Amara gasped, jumping off Ember and picking up the stick before vaulting back on and setting off up the school at a gallop. They were practising something called the litter-picking race but she'd been distracted as she noticed Kalini watching from the fence, her face wistful. Amara could remember how left out she'd felt when she'd first come to the stables and hadn't been part of the squad.

She used the stick to scoop up a plastic container from the ground and then galloped to the end of the school and threw it into a big tub. Ember skidded to a halt beside Cloud and Sirocco, who were ridden by Jasmine and Ollie, the two older riders on the team. They were both fourteen and it was their last year of being able to compete in the local league.

"Are you OK?" Jasmine said, giving Amara a concerned look. "That's the third time you've dropped the stick today and you dropped the bottle in the bottle race."

"I'm fine," said Amara as Imogen and Bea took their turn at the race.

"So how come you keep messing up?" Ollie asked.

"My mind's just on other stuff," Amara said, glancing at Kalini.

"Well, you'd better get it back on mounted games," warned Jasmine. "Jill hates it when people don't concentrate."

"OK, guys, come back to this end!" Jill called as Imogen and Bea completed a perfect handover.

Amara rode back with Jasmine and Ollie. "Good work, you two," Jill said to them, then she turned to Amara. "Amara, you haven't been riding to your full potential today. Next session I want to see you fully focused at all times and I don't want to see you missing your handovers like that again. Understand?"

Amara's cheeks flamed red. "I understand,"

she muttered, staring at Ember's mane.

"Right, the ponies have done enough for today," Jill said briskly. "You can take them in." She turned to Kalini. "Kalini, I've got time to give you a lesson now."

While Kalini got ready, Alex, Imogen and Amara took their ponies for a walk in the woods at the end of the lane to cool them off.

"So, what was up with you?" Imogen asked Amara as they rode through the trees. The track wound up a hill and came out on the ridgeway at the top.

Amara shrugged. She really liked Alex and Imogen but they weren't best friends with Kalini the way she was and she wasn't sure they would understand. "I don't know. I'm probably just tired because of the storm waking me up in the night," she lied.

40

Imogen nodded. "It must have been really bad here." Branches littered the track and the further they went up the hill, the worse the damage became. Tree boughs had fallen and creepers had been ripped from tree trunks.

They rode out on to the ridgeway, the highest point of the steep hill. There was a sheer drop on one side, and near to a spring bubbling out of the rocks they saw a circle of barren ground. Bushes and grass had been ripped up, leaving just the bare earth and stone, and there was a charred forked pattern where lightning had hit the ground. "Whoa, it looks like there was a tornado in this spot," said Alex.

Amara. She heard Ember speaking to her in her thoughts.

Yes.

A storm wouldn't have caused this much damage in just one small area. Unless . . . unless it was a magic storm.

Amara caught her breath.

"What is it?" said Imogen.

"Ember thinks the storm could have been caused by magic," Amara told them.

"But none of our horses could conjure a wind this strong," said Imogen. "Sirocco's a wind horse but he can only conjure short, strong gusts of wind, and anyway, he would never damage the countryside like this."

It wasn't Sirocco, said Ember. *It wasn't any of us.*

Amara felt a cold tingle run down her spine as a horrible thought crept into her mind. "Maybe Ivy's to blame?"

Ivy Thornton was the owner of Storm

Stables, a smart yard just outside Eastwall. She was a Night Rider – a True Rider who had decided to use the elemental horses' powers for her own selfish gains. Her elemental horse, Bolt, had the power of electricity and Ivy wanted to increase her powers by using magic to steal the abilities of other elemental horses. Just a few weeks ago, she had tried to kidnap Ember using a glowing blue halter made from a magical binding rope that forced him to obey her. Luckily, Amara had managed to fight her off.

"Maybe she's stolen a wind horse's power and given it to Bolt," said Imogen in alarm. "A wind horse and Bolt's electric power could conjure up a storm."

"But why would she cause a storm here?" said Alex, looking round at the wind-damaged ridge. "What would be the point?"

"I don't know," said Amara uneasily. "But I think we need to tell Jill what we've found! If it is Ivy, I bet she's up to no good!"

CHAPTER FOUR

Back at the stables, they turned the ponies out in the meadow and ran to the school where Kalini was riding Blue. She was cantering around and riding really well. For a moment, Amara forgot about the wind damage on the hill and felt a rush of hope. If Kalini could impress Jill then maybe she would let her try out for the squad!

"Would you like to have a go over a jump?" Jill called to Kalini.

To Amara's surprise, Kalini shook her head. "I haven't really done much jumping."

"No problem," said Jill. "We can build up to jumping. You've done really well today."

"Jill! Jill! We need to talk to you!" Alex called impatiently as Kalini dismounted. "It's about . . ." Imogen elbowed him and looked meaningfully at Kalini. ". . . stuff!" he finished.

Jill turned to Kalini. "Are you all right to untack Blue on your own?"

"Yes, sure," said Kalini, shooting a curious look at Alex, Imogen and Amara.

She led Blue out of the school and Jill came over to the fence. "What's the matter?"

They told her about the storm damage on the hill.

"Do you think Ivy did it?" said Amara.

Jill frowned. "I can't see why she would do something like that. But then again after her attempt to kidnap Ember, who knows what she'll try next."

"We'll keep a watch out for anything else weird," said Imogen.

"There's no way she's going to hurt any of our horses!" Alex said.

"Someone wants to hurt the horses?" They jumped and saw that Kalini had walked up behind them without them hearing her.

"It's nothing to worry about, Kalini," Jill said quickly. "Now," she added briskly, "Please can you all put the jumps away?"

Whispering together, Alex and Imogen hurried to the far side of the school. Kalini followed Amara to a closer jump. "What was all that about?" she asked curiously. "What

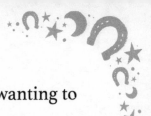

did Alex mean about someone wanting to hurt the horses?"

"It's nothing," said Amara quickly.

Kalini frowned. "It didn't sound like nothing."

"It really isn't anything to worry about," Amara said awkwardly.

"So why won't you tell me?" pushed Kalini.

"I can't," Amara said. "It's just something about . . . to do with mounted games." She blushed as Kalini gave her a disbelieving look. "Come on, let's move this jump."

"Fine," Kalini said, sounding hurt. "I guess you think I won't understand because I don't know much about mounted games."

"It's not that . . ." Amara started to say, but Kalini was already carrying a pole away to the side of the school.

To Amara's relief, Kalini didn't stay in a mood with her and by the time they went back to Amara's house that evening for their sleepover, the conversation at the stables seemed to have been forgotten. Amara lived in a cottage near where the lane joined the main road. It had pretty purple wisteria growing up one side of the doorway and had a pear tree in the front garden. Amara couldn't wait to try the pears but they wouldn't be ready until the early autumn.

"So, who's for home-made pizza?" Amara's dad said as they washed their hands.

"Me!" they both shouted.

Mr Thompson got the pizza dough and

toppings out of the fridge and they piled their pizzas high – pepperoni, peppers and sweetcorn for Amara, and olives, peppers and mushrooms for Kalini. Then they went outside and while the pizzas cooked they put up three jumps using buckets and gardening equipment from the shed and jumped round it, pretending to ride horses.

"And here comes Kalini Batra on Prince,"

said Kalini, being the commentator as she cantered towards the first jump. "But oh no, he's being naughty." She pretended to rear. "Can Kalini control him? Come on, Prince and Kalini! You can do it!" She leapt over the row of plant pots and then jumped the remaining obstacles. "What a round!" she exclaimed, patting her imaginary pony.

Amara giggled. "You'll have to jump for real next time you have a lesson with Jill," she said to Kalini. "Why didn't you today?"

Kalini shrugged. "I've not really jumped much before."

"So? Jill will teach you," said Amara. "You have to try and impress her so she'll invite you to join the games squad."

Kalini looked dubious. "Me? I'm not a good enough rider for that."

"You are!" insisted Amara.

Kalini shook her head. "I'm really not. I thought you were all amazing when I watched you today."

"I'm only good because of Ember," said Amara. She chose her words carefully. "If you're with the right pony, it's much easier. Maybe you could ask Jill if you can ride Forest or Sparks?"

"I'm happy with Blue," said Kalini.

Amara continued trying to convince her but nothing she said changed Kalini's mind. She really wasn't very confident about her riding.

If only I could tell her about the elemental horses then she'd understand why it's so important to impress Jill, Amara thought. *And if she became a True Rider then I know her horse would help her feel braver and more confident, just like Ember helps me.* Her mind turned it over. If only there was something she could do!

Amara tried to keep thoughts of Kalini becoming a True Rider out of her mind as the friends spent the evening doing online pony quizzes, which Kalini won, and making up a game with Amara's model ponies. They had an early midnight feast of sweets and popcorn and then fell asleep, tired out after the busy day.

But in the night, Amara woke up to the sound of the wind rattling the windowpanes. The trees in the garden were creaking and there was the sound of bangs and crashes as things fell over.

It's another storm, she realised. *I hope the*

ponies are doing OK.

A high-pitched whinny cut through the sound of the wind. Amara sat up, alarm flickering through her. It sounded like a horse was in the lane outside her house. *Maybe one of the Moonlight Stables ponies had broken out of their field?* Getting up and stepping over Kalini, who was asleep in a sleeping bag on the floor, she went to her window and looked out.

The trees were whipping from side to side in the strong wind and clouds were sweeping across the moon and the stars. Kalini turned over in her sleeping bag and started muttering in her sleep. From the window, Amara could see out into the lane. She heard the faint clatter of hooves and for a moment she thought she saw the shadowy shape of a

 horse galloping past her house. She blinked, but the horse had gone. *Had she really seen it?* Looking out, all she could see was the windswept front garden and the empty lane again. *I must have imagined it,* she thought.

She waited a few moments longer then padded back to bed. But as she snuggled down under the covers, she was sure she heard the faint sound of whinnying again.

"Did you hear that storm last night?" asked Amara's mum when they went down for breakfast in the morning.

"Yes, it woke me up," said Amara, putting some bread in the toaster.

"There was nothing in the weather forecast about it," said her mum. "It was completely unexpected. Dad's outside tidying up. Some tiles came off the roof."

"I hope the ponies are OK," Kalini said.

"We should go and check," said Amara. "Is that all right, Mum?"

"Sure, take your toast with you," she said.

The girls set off down the lane, eating their toast as they went. Bins had been knocked over and a tree in one of the neighbours' gardens had been uprooted and fallen through a fence.

Just as they reached the stables, a smart black car drew up behind them. Alex and Imogen jumped out. "See you later, Mum!" Alex said.

"Thanks for the lift!" called Imogen as she shut her door.

They ran over to join Amara and Kalini. "What are you doing here so early?" Amara asked.

"My mum heard on the radio that there had been another storm over this way," said Imogen. "We thought we'd come and—"

"Check on the ponies," Alex interrupted. "Come on!"

He ran down the lane to where there was a small gate that led into the meadow. Imogen hurried after him.

"If they're going to check on the ponies,

maybe we should go and help Jill," Kalini said, looking up the drive to the yard where they could see Jill picking up tiles that had fallen from the stable roof.

"Um . . ." Amara hesitated, looking between the meadow and the yard. She really wanted to see if Ember was OK.

"Amara!" Imogen shouted frantically from the gate, her face pale. "Some of the ponies have gone!"

CHAPTER FIVE

Ember had gone! Amara sprinted towards the meadow.

"I'll go and tell Jill!" Kalini shouted, running up the drive.

Imogen and Amara scrambled over the gate and ran into the meadow. Cloud, Sirocco, Forest, Sparks and Sandy were gathered together, their ears pricked as they looked towards the field where the riding school ponies were kept, but Ember, Rose and Tide were nowhere to be seen.

Amara's heart pounded. Had Ivy taken them? But then Alex yelled, "There they are! It's OK."

Amara followed where he was pointing and saw Ember, Tide and Rose in the next field, standing in front of a gap in the fence that separated the riding school ponies' field from the lane. A section of the wooden posts and rails had blown down and the elemental horses were stopping the riding school ponies from getting out. Relief hit Amara like a tidal wave.

She raced across the meadow, climbed through the fence between the elemental ponies' and the riding school ponies' fields and ran over to Ember. "Oh, Ember! I thought you'd been stolen!" she said, flinging her arms around his neck.

He nuzzled her. *The fence blew down in the wind and we wanted to stop the ponies going out on to the road.*

Amara remembered the horse she'd seen in the night. *Are they all still here? Did any escape?*

No, they're all safe, Ember told her.

She kissed him. She must have imagined the pony in the night. *I'm so glad. That storm was wild, wasn't it?*

Y . . . yes.

Amara heard him hesitate. *What is it, Ember?*

It didn't feel like a normal storm, he said slowly. *I could sense magic in the rain.*

Magic? Amara felt a prickle of alarm.

Ember nodded. *And the air felt different.*

62

Like it was sharp – electric . . .

"Hey, you two, we should catch the
riding school ponies and take them to their
stables!" Imogen called, interrupting Amara
and Ember's conversation. She and Alex had
fetched the headcollars from by the gate.
The ponies were happy to be caught – all
apart from Bella, a very round, greedy pony,
who was enjoying the grass far too much.
Whenever they went near her, she trotted
away.

"I'll get her!" said Alex. He started to run
towards Bella. "Come here, Bella!"

Bella bucked cheekily and broke into a
canter. Alex chased her but she was much
faster than him.

"You're just making her worse, Alex!"
shouted Imogen. She pulled a carrot out

of her pocket. "Here, Bella, look, I've got a yummy carrot. Do you want it?" She waggled the carrot. Bella pricked her ears and trotted over.

"See," Imogen called smugly to Alex. "This is how you catch a pony— Oh!" she gasped as Bella snatched the carrot and cantered away.

Alex hooted with laughter. "I think you mean that's how you don't catch a pony!"

"Hey, guys!" Kalini was coming across the field with a feed bucket and headcollar. "I told Jill but she already knew about Ember, Tide and Rose. She said she'd seen them in here, keeping the others safe." She looked impressed. "I didn't know ponies could be quite so smart."

Amara exchanged knowing looks with Imogen and Alex.

"Mounted games ponies are very clever," said Imogen hastily.

"Anyway, Jill said to bring the riding school ponies in," Kalini continued. "I'll try catching Bella with this."

Putting the headcollar behind her back, she rattled the feed in the bucket. The little pony pricked her ears. Kalini approached her slowly and then stopped, turning her body sideways so that she wasn't looking directly at her. She rattled the feed again. Bella started to walk over.

Kalini waited patiently until the pony came all the way up to her and then as Bella put her head in the bucket she slipped the headcollar over her nose. "Good girl," she praised. Bella's ears flickered happily as she munched.

"Now that's how you catch a pony!" Alex said, elbowing Imogen.

Imogen grinned. "Kalini, you were great!" she called.

"Thanks," Kalini said, looking pleased. "I read about catching difficult ponies in a book. It was fun to try it out."

They led the ponies to the yard and Ember, Tide and Rose jumped back over the fence into their own meadow.

"Awesome!" breathed Kalini. "They really

are the cleverest ponies ever."

Amara hid her smile. If only she knew!

There was even more damage on the yard
than the day before – tiles had fallen from
the roof and Jill's hanging baskets had been
scattered across the yard.

"I hope that's the last storm," said Imogen
as she and Amara swept up the flowers and
soil.

Amara remembered what Ember had said
to her in the field. "It might not be," she
said. "Ember said he felt magic in the air last
night."

Imogen gave her a quick look. "Tide said
that to me too."

Alex spotted them whispering. "What are you talking about?" he asked, leaving Kalini collecting tiles.

They filled him in.

"If the horses are right then maybe it is Ivy causing the storms like we thought," Amara said in a low voice. "Ember did say that the air felt electric."

"And her stable is called Storm Stables after all!" added Alex. "We should try and find out."

"But how?" said Imogen.

Alex grinned. "Ivy has spied on Moonlight Stables before, so now I reckon it's our turn to spy on her!"

"That could be dangerous," said Imogen uncertainly.

"But if it is Ivy, we need to stop her," said

Amara. The others nodded.

"Let's ask Jill if we can take the ponies out for a ride at lunchtime," Alex suggested. "Then we can ride to Storm Stables and see what they're up to." He looked at them eagerly. "What do you think?"

Before they could answer, Kalini joined them. "What are you all talking about?"

"We're going to ask Jill if we can take Tide, Rose and Ember out for a hack," said Imogen.

"Do you think she'll let me come with you on Blue?" Kalini asked hopefully.

Amara's heart sank.

"I don't think you'll be allowed, Kalini," said Imogen, looking uncomfortable. "No one's allowed to take the riding school ponies out without an adult."

"But Jill lets you take the games ponies out?" Kalini frowned. "That doesn't make sense. Why is it one rule for them and another for the other ponies?"

"That's just the way it is." Alex fidgeted awkwardly. "Sorry, Kalini, but you can't come."

Amara saw hurt flash across Kalini's eyes. "I won't go," Amara said quickly. She really wanted to but she didn't want Kalini to feel left out. "I'll stay here."

"No. You should go," Kalini said. She saw Amara was about to argue. "I mean it," she insisted. "It's not like you're going to be out all day. It's only for an hour or so. I'll be fine."

"Are you sure?" Amara asked.

"Positive," Kalini replied.

Amara gave her a small smile and then

70

went with Alex and Imogen to find Jill. Luckily she didn't ask why they wanted to hack over to Storm Stables. "But only go to the outside," Jill warned. "You mustn't take horses on to other yards uninvited, magical or not."

Amara couldn't help feeling bad as they rode out, leaving Kalini behind. She was quiet as the other two chatted and joked.

Are you all right, Amara? Ember asked.

She stroked his neck. *It's so hard not being able to tell Kalini about the elemental horses. I don't like keeping secrets from her.* Amara swallowed. She'd been so excited about Kalini helping at Moonlight Stables but she hadn't thought about the problems it would cause. Then Ember leapt forward after the other ponies and Amara gratefully

71

lost herself in the rush of speed and the pounding of his hooves.

After half an hour's riding, they arrived at Storm Stables, approaching on a bridlepath that ran through the fields behind the yard. They halted in a small wood next to the parking area where they could watch without being seen. Amara had heard a lot about Storm Stables but she hadn't been there before. From their vantage point in the woods, she could see it had big black electric gates with spikes on the top, a large parking area with gleaming horseboxes and a building which had a sign saying *Office and Tack Shop*. The horses were stabled in a modern barn that was painted black and there was an indoor school as well as jumping and dressage arenas. Two smartly dressed grooms were sweeping the spotless yard while a woman was heading into the tack shop.

"We're not going to find out much just watching from here," said Alex. "We should have a look around."

"But Jill said we mustn't," said Imogen.

"No, she said we mustn't take the ponies on to the yard." Alex dismounted. "She didn't say we couldn't go in."

"You shouldn't go on your own," said Amara. Alex often acted without thinking. "I'll come with you – if you don't mind holding the ponies?" she said to Imogen.

"Fine. But don't do anything stupid, either of you," Imogen warned.

"As if we would!" Alex said, with a grin.

Imogen groaned.

There was a gap in the fence to give the Storm Stables riders access to the bridlepath and fields. Amara and Alex walked cautiously into the parking area. There was no one around. Amara couldn't help comparing it to the cheerful bustle of Moonlight Stables. As they got closer to the wall of the indoor school they heard voices inside.

"Faster, Daniela!"

"Go, Shannon! Make this one count!"

"That sounds like a mounted games practice," Alex hissed to Amara. "But Storm Stables don't have a games team."

"Maybe Ivy started one when Zara and Daniela moved here," Amara whispered back.

Zara and Daniela, who were cousins, had been in Jill's mounted games squad when Amara had first started helping at Moonlight

Stables. Daniela had ridden Sparks and Zara had ridden Ember. Neither girl had been chosen to be True Riders but they knew about the elemental horses' secret because their grandfather had been a True Rider. They had been really mean to Amara, laughing at her for wearing old riding clothes. When Ember had chosen Amara to be his True Rider, Zara had been so furious that she and Daniela had left and gone to Storm Stables instead.

Alex ran to the side of the indoor school to look through the gaps in the wooden slats of the wall.

"Alex! What are you doing?" hissed Amara, looking round anxiously, hoping no one would come out and see him.

Alex beckoned her over. "It is a games

team!" he hissed. "Look!"

Heart pounding, she joined him. Peering through the slats, she could see two boys practising weaving in and out of a line of poles on their ponies while Zara, Daniela and Shannon watched. The three girls were mounted on stunning ponies with glossy coats, long thick manes and tails and very intelligent expressions. Zara's was a fiery chestnut with a white blaze; Daniela's was a stockier bright bay with a glossy coat

and black mane and tail; and Shannon's was a dark grey with a pure white mane and tail. *Elemental horses,* thought Amara immediately. But although they were beautiful, all three ponies looked mean and kept threatening to bite each other as they stood side by side. The ponies the two boys were riding were fast but Amara didn't think they were elemental horses. She watched as the boys raced each other down the two lines of poles, finishing neck and neck.

"Wow, they're good!" Amara whispered as the boys high-fived each other.

"Lorenzo Holt and Duncan Packwood," Alex whispered back. "They ride for the county team. They didn't keep their ponies at Storm Stables before. I bet Ivy bribed them to come here and join her new team."

Amara nodded, remembering how Ivy had once tried to convince her to take Ember to Storm Stables, promising her all the latest riding gear if she did.

"Let's go and look round some more," said Alex, tugging at her sleeve.

They crept away from the school and headed for the barn where the horses were kept. It was spotless inside, the black doors gleaming and headcollars hanging on their hooks, leadropes neatly coiled. There was a large dapple-grey horse in the first stall. Instinctively, Amara went to pat it but had to jump back as it flattened its ears and swung its teeth at her.

The horses here are as mean as Ivy and her riders, Amara thought.

"Amara, look, it's the tack room." Alex was standing in the doorway of a large room. "And they've got a wall chart showing the top riders of the week."

Joining him, Amara saw a pyramid of rider photos with Zara's picture on the top. "Imagine if Jill did that!" she said.

A voice snapped out behind them. "If she did, you might all be better riders!"

Amara's heart leapt into her throat. Ivy Thornton was standing in the barn entrance. She was wearing a white shirt and black breeches and her dark hair was pulled back in a low bun. Her pale blue eyes glittered and she tapped her riding crop threateningly against the side of one of her long riding boots as she walked towards them. "I take trespassing very seriously, you know." Her voice was low but charged with menace.

Amara's heart beat wildly. She glanced around but there was no other way out. She and Alex were trapped!

CHAPTER SIX

"We're not trespassing!" Alex said quickly.
"We're here to . . . to visit the shop!"

"Oh, really?" Ivy's arched eyebrows rose.
"And you just happened to wander into the
barn by mistake."

"Yes," said Alex.

"We weren't sure where the shop was,"
added Amara, her mouth feeling as dry as
sandpaper.

"If you've come shopping, where's your

money?" The words snapped out of Ivy's mouth.

To Amara's surprise, Alex reached into his pocket for his phone and pulled a twenty pound note out from his phone case. "Here."

Ivy looked taken aback.

"So if you could just tell us the way to the shop," Alex went on, "that would be great." He sidled past her, pulling Amara with him. "Oh yes, there it is!" he said as they reached the barn entrance. "Silly us! I don't know how we missed it. I'd better go and buy that hoof pick I wanted!"

Ivy stepped towards them, hissing, "You two are not going anywhere . . ." She broke off as the smart woman they had seen earlier came out of the shop with two full carrier bags and sent them all a curious look.

Amara seized the opportunity. "Come on, Alex!" she gasped.

"Maybe I'll buy that hoof pick another day!" Alex called back to Ivy as they sprinted across the yard. They didn't stop running until they were through the gap in the fence and safely back in the woods.

"You were ages! What happened? I saw you go into the barn and then I saw Ivy go in too!" exclaimed Imogen. "I was just about to leave the ponies and come after you."

Alex grinned. "It was awesome! She almost caught us but we escaped!"

Amara wasn't sure she would have described it as awesome. Her legs felt shaky and her heart was still racing. "I'm so glad we got away," she said, giving Ember a hug. "How come you had twenty pounds, Alex?"

Alex shrugged. "Mum just likes me to carry emergency money." Amara was astonished. Even on her birthday the most money she had ever been given was ten pounds, and her mum usually looked after it until there was something she wanted to buy. She couldn't imagine having a twenty pound note just in case she needed it.

Amara! There's someone coming! Ember said warningly.

Hearing hoofbeats, she swung round and saw Zara, Daniela and Shannon burst into the woods from a hidden path. They were on their elemental horses.

Alex vaulted on to Rose. "Let's go!"

"You three are not going anywhere!" said Zara icily. "Ivy told us to find out why you came here, so you're not leaving until we have some answers."

"How exactly do you plan on stopping us?" said Alex.

"I was hoping you'd ask that. Show them, Scorch!" Zara ordered. The chestnut horse she was riding stamped her hooves and shot a small ball of flames straight in front of Rose's hooves. Rose hastily backed away as it exploded into sparks and then sizzled out.

Amara could feel tension flowing through Ember. She knew he was longing to use his magic but she hoped he wouldn't. He was a far more powerful fire horse than Scorch and although she didn't like the three girls, she didn't want them to be hurt. "Let us pass!" she demanded.

"No. We want answers first!" said Daniela. "Your turn, Quake!" Quake, the bay pony she was riding, stamped his large hooves and the ground they were standing on trembled and shook. The ponies whinnied in alarm as they tried to stay on their feet. Daniela, Zara and Shannon laughed.

"So why did you come here? Were you trying to spy on us before the competition?" Zara said.

"The competition?" echoed Alex in

surprise. "No. We came because we wanted to find out why Ivy's been causing magical storms up on the hill by our yard!"

Amara saw the three Storm Stables girls frown.

"What are you going on about?" said Daniela.

Alex rolled his eyes. "Don't pretend you don't know."

Daniela's frown deepened. "We don't—"

"Uh – yes! Of course we know about the storms!" said Zara, cutting across her cousin. "Yeah, that's what Ivy's been doing, isn't it? Causing magic storms at Moonlight Stables." She shot pointed looks at Daniela and Shannon, who nodded quickly.

"But why would she—" Alex broke off with a gasp. "I've got it! She wants to sabotage our games team by injuring our ponies! That's it, isn't it?"

"Yeah, that's exactly it," Zara said swiftly.

Daniela gave a mean laugh. "Though I don't know why she's bothering. After all, Amara's bound to fall off."

Zara smirked. "With her on your team you've got no hope!"

Amara felt fierce anger suddenly surge through Ember. He reared up and banged his front hooves down furiously. "Ember, no!" Amara cried as a huge fireball shot straight at the Storm Stables ponies.

To her relief, they cantered out of the way just in time. The fireball hit the ground, exploding into burning flames.

Seeming to realise that Ember was too upset to control his magic, Tide instantly stamped her hooves and a sheet of rain fell down, drenching the flames – and Zara, Shannon and Daniela at the same time.

They shrieked and spluttered.

Alex burst out laughing. "Serves you right for being mean about Amara!"

Amara could still feel Ember trembling with anger. Not wanting him to lose his temper again, she urged him past Zara, Shannon and Daniela while they were wiping the rain off their faces.

"That's it, run away back to your lame stables with your rubbish team!" sneered Zara, water dripping down her nose.

"Just wait till the competition; we'll destroy you!" said Shannon.

Amara felt Ember stiffen and start to turn. "Please don't, Ember," she begged. She stroked his neck. "Stay calm."

It's hard to, he told her.

I know, she said, encouraging him away from the three girls. *They're really annoying and mean but you can't use magic to hurt them. That would be wrong.*

You're right, he said reluctantly. *I shouldn't have lost my temper. Sorry, Amara. I just hate it when people are horrible to you.*

That's OK. She hugged him.

"So," Alex said, once they were safely away from Storm Stables. "We were right. The storms are magical and Ivy is causing them."

Imogen nodded. "Because she wants to try and stop us competing."

Amara remembered the confusion she'd seen on Zara, Daniela and Shannon's faces when Alex mentioned the storms. "Do you really think that? It looked to me like they didn't know about the storms."

"Zara admitted it," said Alex. "She said that was what Ivy was doing."

"Mmm," Amara said, not fully convinced.

Amara? She heard the question from Ember's thoughts.

Yes?

I think you're right. The horses seemed surprised too when Alex mentioned about the storms. Zara could have been lying when she said Ivy caused them.

But why would she do that?

I don't know, but I'm sure there's something else going on, Ember said.

Amara nodded and, feeling very uneasy, she followed the others home.

CHAPTER SEVEN

Kalini was watching out for them when they arrived back. "Did you have a good ride?" she said cheerfully as she helped Amara untack.

"Mmm," Amara said, her mind on the conversation she and Ember had been having on the way home.

"What did you do? Did you go for lots of canters?"

"It was just a ride!" Amara said abruptly.

She could have kicked herself as she saw

Kalini's face fall. "Sorry," she said. "I didn't mean to snap."

Kalini nodded but continued helping her untack in silence. Amara felt awful. It wasn't Kalini's fault that she didn't know the purpose of the ride and that she didn't know how stressful it had been. "Oh, Kalini, I wish you could be a—" Amara stopped with the words True Rider hanging on her lips. "Be . . . on the games squad," she finished. "Why don't you ask Jill if you can ride Sparks in your lesson today?"

Kalini looked uncertain. "He looks very strong and he seems quite lively. I don't think I'm a good enough rider for him."

"You are!" said Amara. "Daniela used to ride him and you're just as good as she is!" It wasn't exactly true. Daniela had been riding since she was little and was very experienced, but Amara's longing for Kalini to be a True Rider made her stretch the truth. "You'll be OK. I know you will. Ask if you can ride him. Please!"

Kalini hesitated for a moment and then nodded. "OK. If you're sure I'm good enough."

"I am," Amara said in delight. "Let's ask Jill."

Jill didn't seem convinced at first but after some persuasion she agreed that Kalini could try Sparks out.

Amara, Imogen and Alex watched from the fence. Sparks was a pony who loved to go fast and he was clearly excited to be out with a new rider. When Jill told Kalini to walk him round the school, he jogged and sidled sideways. Looking worried, Kalini shortened her reins.

"Don't have your reins too tight; he'll only fight against you!" called Jill as Sparks shook his head. "Try and relax, Kalini. That will help him relax too."

But as Sparks pranced, Kalini tightened the reins even more. Fighting against the hold on his mouth, the bay-and-white pony threw his head hard between his legs, pulling the reins out of Kalini's hands. Realising his head was suddenly free, he leapt forward. Kalini cried out in alarm and tried to grab at his reins but she couldn't gather them up in time and he set off at a canter.

"Kalini, get hold of the reins and sit back!" shouted Jill.

But in her fear, Kalini seemed to have

forgotten everything she knew about riding. She leant forward instead, grabbing Sparks's mane.

Sparks was trained to go faster when someone leant forward and so he sped up.

Kalini shrieked in alarm. Amara felt a stab of fear as Sparks galloped round the school. If Kalini fell off at such a speed, she was going to hurt herself. *What have I done?*

she thought. *It's my fault she's riding him. I should have listened!*

"Steady, Sparks!" Jill spoke soothingly but firmly as she strode across the school to block his path. "There's a good boy. Whoa now." Sparks came to an abrupt stop in front of her and Kalini flew off into the sand.

"Kalini!" Amara scrambled over the fence and raced to where Kalini was starting to sit up.

"Are you all right?" said Jill anxiously.

"I'm fine," Kalini muttered, looking very embarrassed as she jumped to her feet, brushing the sand off her.

"Well, I think it's clear that Sparks isn't the pony for you," said Jill. "Let's get you back on Blue." Kalini nodded. "Imogen and Alex, can you take Sparks in and untack him while I

get Blue out for Kalini?"

"Sure!" they both said.

"I'm glad you're all right," Alex said to Kalini as they hurried to get Sparks.

Kalini didn't reply. She still looked mortified.

They led Sparks away and Jill went to fetch Blue, leaving Amara and Kalini alone together.

Amara felt awful. "Oh, Kalini! I'm ... I'm sorry I got you to ride Sparks," she said as soon as they were on their own.

"You told me I was good enough!" Kalini burst out angrily. "You told me he'd be fine! Now I feel like a total idiot!"

"Everyone falls off sometimes. No one thinks you're an idiot."

"Well, I do!" Tears sprang to Kalini's eyes

and she turned her face away.

"Kalini . . ." Amara put a hand on her arm.

"No!" Kalini shook her off angrily. "Leave me alone, Amara!" She marched off to the side of the school and stood there, her arms folded, her shoulders hunched.

Amara didn't know what to do. Kalini was normally really calm and Amara had never seen her lose her temper before. She stood awkwardly in the middle of the school and felt very relieved when Jill came back with Blue.

"Here, hop on Blue," Jill called to Kalini. "He'll look after you."

Kalini walked over to her, still avoiding Amara's eyes.

Amara went back to the fence to watch. Every time Kalini rode past her she tried to give her an encouraging smile but Kalini looked pointedly away. Amara's heart sank. She really hoped Kalini would forgive her soon.

Kalini's lesson on Blue went well but she still wouldn't talk to Amara when she got off. Their argument was boiling and seething in Amara's mind as she joined the others for a training session on Ember. She found it even harder to concentrate than she had done the day before, making stupid mistakes.

Alex lost his temper after she dropped the litter picking stick for the third time. "Amara, you're being useless!" he yelled at her. "We're definitely going to lose on Saturday!"

"Alex! That's enough!" snapped Jill. "I will not have members of my squad talking to each other like that. Take Rose in and cool down. You're not doing any more riding today."

Glaring at Amara, Alex dismounted and stomped across the school with Rose.

Amara felt her eyes sting with tears. Now Alex was cross with her too! Jill came over. Her voice was gentle but also firm. "Amara, I don't know what's the matter with you at the moment," she said, "but you are really going to have to pull yourself together. If you continue to ride like this, I'm going to have to pull you from the competition. Understand?"

Amara didn't dare speak because she knew she would start to cry. She nodded, a tear falling from one eye.

Jill saw it and her expression softened. "Look, take Ember out for a ride in the woods. I don't think there's any point in you doing more today. We'll have some extra practices in the week and see how you do then."

Feeling the rest of the team's eyes burning into her, Amara rode Ember out of the school.

As soon as they were away from the yard and in the safety of the woods, she dismounted. Putting her arms round his neck, she buried her face in his mane. *Oh, Ember, I've messed*

everything up. Kalini hates me. Alex is mad at me. Jill is going to pull me from the competition. Everyone's cross with me now!

He turned his head and nuzzled her shoulder. *I'm not.*

She took a trembling breath, feeling slightly better. At least she still had him.

You only persuaded Kalini to ride Sparks because you wanted her to be a True Rider and not to feel left out, he said. *It might have worked. You didn't know she would fall.*

I know, but I should have listened to her when she said she didn't want to ride him. I hope she'll forgive me.

I'm sure she will, said Ember. *Just say sorry.*

Amara managed a small smile. *You're right. I'll say sorry again and again until she believes me. And I'll also try really hard not to be so distracted next time we have a training session so that Jill lets me ride in the competition.* She hugged him tightly. *Oh, Ember, I don't know what I'd do without you.*

He snorted softly. *You'll never have to find out.*

Amara swallowed. *I almost did when Ivy tried to kidnap you. What if she's got some other horrible plan and that's why she's conjuring the storms? It could be nothing to do with the games competition.*

Whatever she's got planned, we'll stop her, Ember reassured her. *You, me and the other horses and their True Riders. We're a team.*

Her heart swelled with love. He was right. They were.

"We won't let her win," she whispered.

Never, he replied.

CHAPTER EIGHT

Another storm raged that night but Jill texted them all in the morning to let them know the ponies were fine. Amara felt her tummy twisting itself into knots as she got ready for school. She wondered how Kalini and Alex would be with her that day. She'd texted Kalini five times in the evening but she hadn't replied even though Amara could see she'd read the texts.

Amara was walking into the playground

feeling rather nervous when she heard Alex calling her name.

He came bounding up to her with Imogen and gave her a sheepish grin. "Hey."

"Hi," Amara said warily.

"Go on," Imogen told him, poking him. "Apologise."

Alex rolled his eyes at her. "OK, OK." He turned to Amara. "Sorry, Amara. I shouldn't have got mad at you yesterday."

Imogen shook her head at Alex. "You're such a doughnut."

"I know," Alex said to Amara. "I have this thing called ADHD which means I often do and say things without thinking them through. I try not to lose my temper but sometimes it just happens."

"It's OK," said Amara, feeling very relieved

that he wanted to be friends again. "I shouldn't have dropped the stick so many times."

"Oh no, no, no," Imogen broke in. "Don't give him an excuse. He shouldn't have yelled at you like that no matter what you did!"

"She's right. I really am sorry. Friends again?" Alex said hopefully to Amara.

"Friends again," she told him, smiling.

Unfortunately, Kalini didn't seem so keen to make up. Amara tried saying sorry to her several times but Kalini just ignored her.

Amara was very glad when home-time came. Her dad picked her up and when he parked the car outside the cottage, she noticed that dark clouds were starting to gather overhead. "It looks like there's going to be another storm!" he said. "We're not going to have any tiles left on the roof at this rate!"

Amara felt worry prickle through her. By the time she had dinner and got changed out of her school uniform, the sky had darkened and rain was hammering down. *Jill might need help. I'll ask Dad if I can go to the stables,* she thought, looking out of the window. But just then she saw a figure in a pink coat cycle past her house battling against the rain and wind. It was Kalini.

Amara changed her mind. She didn't want to go to the stables if Kalini was there. She'd had enough of feeling guilty all day at school.

She went into the lounge and put the TV on but she couldn't focus on it. She kept glancing out of the window and thinking about the ponies, a sense of dread creeping through her. She had a strong feeling that something was wrong. Outside, a garden chair fell over with a crash. Then her phone buzzed and she saw a text from Imogen.

What's the weather like with you?

Really stormy. The worst yet! Amara typed back.

I'm going to ask Dad if he'll drive me to the yard so I can help with the ponies. I'll see if Alex can come too xx

Amara made up her mind. Her argument with Kalini wasn't as important as making sure the ponies were safe. She typed a reply.

I'll see you there xx

Five minutes later, Amara ran on to the yard, the gale buffeting against her. She had to jump out of the way as a bucket came rolling across the ground. Grabbing hold of it, she ran to the feed room. As she undid the bolt, the wind grabbed the door from her, slamming it back against the wall. Amara shoved the bucket inside and hauled the door shut with both hands.

She heard hooves and saw Jill coming down the yard, leading her horse, Apollo. The bay thoroughbred had his head bent against the wind. "Amara, what are you doing here?" Jill shouted, trying to make herself heard above the wind.

"I came to help," Amara shouted back.

"Thanks!" Jill gave her Apollo's leadrope and pulled the stable door open. Amara led

him in and helped Jill pull the door shut,
bolting both the top and bottom halves of it
to keep the rain out.

"Where's Kalini?" Amara asked.

Jill looked surprised. "Kalini? I haven't seen
her."

Amara frowned. Maybe the person she'd
seen on the bike hadn't been Kalini after all.

"Can you give me a hand getting Blue and
Pippin in?" Jill shouted.

They battled their way up the field and
fetched the two ponies in. Once they were
both safely inside their stables, Jill turned to
Amara. "That's the riding school ponies safe.
The elemental horses will be fine. They'll
just stay put if their fence blows down."

"Alex and Imogen should be here in a
minute," said Amara. "Is there anything

else you want us to do?"

"No, everything's done. You should all go home and get inside where it's safe and warm."

Amara said goodbye and headed down to the gate. Alex and Imogen were fighting their way up the drive. The wind was whipping Imogen's pigtails around and they both had their coats pulled tightly around them.

"Everything's done here," Amara shouted. "Jill said to go home, but you can come back to mine if your dad's gone home."

"OK, but first I want to see the ponies," said Imogen. "I've got a weird feeling."

"Me too," said Alex. "It's like there's something wrong."

Amara felt a chill run through her. It was exactly how she'd been feeling.

They made their way down the lane to the meadow, the wind growing stronger by the minute. The eight ponies were standing around anxiously. As soon as Ember, Rose and Tide saw them they galloped over.

Amara, I'm so glad you're here, said Ember. *I'm sure something magical is happening up on the hill. I keep hearing whinnying and the air feels wrong, kind of prickly and sharp.*

"Guys, Tide says there's something going on up on the hill!" shouted Imogen.

"Rose says that too," said Alex. "She thinks there's a horse there. She heard hoofbeats last night and can hear whinnying now."

Amara vaulted on to Ember. "We need to find out what's going on up there. Who's going to come with me?"

"Me!" Imogen and Alex said together.

Can you hear the whinnying, Amara?
Ember asked as they cantered up the hill
through the swaying trees.

No, she told him.

But it's really loud.

*Maybe if it's a magic horse, only other
magical horses can hear it?* said Amara. *Do
you think it's Bolt, Ivy's horse?*

I don't know, he said as they cantered
around a tree. *I don't get the feeling it's her
but—*

"Ember, careful!" Amara gasped as
she spotted a figure ahead of them. She
recognised the bright pink coat and long
dark ponytail instantly. "Kalini! What are
you doing out here?"

Kalini's eyes widened as she saw them.
"Where's your tack and what are you all

doing out in this weather?"

"We ... um ... sometimes ride without saddles and bridles," Amara said quickly.

"Yes, it's good practice for improving our balance for games," said Imogen.

"You're telling me you've come out here in a storm because you're trying to improve your balance?" Kalini looked like she didn't believe a word they said.

"Forget it for now," said Alex. "What are you doing here, Kalini?"

"I was on my way to the stables and heard a horse whinnying. It sounded distressed. I've been searching for it in the woods," said Kalini, glancing round anxiously. "There it is again. Can you hear it?"

Amara couldn't. Imogen and Alex both shook their heads as well.

"You must be able to hear it. It's coming from up there!" exclaimed Kalini, pointing towards the ridgeway. "We've got to help it!" She set off.

Amara didn't know what to do. It was clear to her there was no way Kalini was going to go back at this point but if it was an elemental horse they couldn't let her see it.

"Kalini! Wait! Maybe you should go home," called Imogen, clearly thinking the same thing.

"No way," said Kalini stubbornly.

What should we do, Ember? Amara thought.

She can ride with you, Ember said. *I'm strong enough to carry you both.*

But what if it's an elemental horse? What if it's Bolt with Ivy?

Just bring her. I think we should.

Amara hesitated but she trusted Ember. If he thought they should take Kalini then she wasn't going to argue any more. "Kalini, you can ride Ember with me," she said, ignoring the alarmed looks the others gave her. She rode to a fallen tree. "Here, get on!"

Kalini stepped on to the trunk and climbed on to Ember's back in front of Amara. Amara tried not to sit too far back where horses' backs were weakest.

Is that OK? she asked Ember.

That's fine, he said.

He started climbing up the hillside, his muscles working hard as he struggled against the force of the wind. Imogen and Alex rode up alongside Amara.

"What are we going to do about her?" Alex

mouthed, pointing at Kalini.

"What if Ivy's there?" mouthed Imogen, looking panicked.

Unfortunately, Kalini chose that moment to glance back over her shoulder and caught them in their silent conversation. "What's going on?" she demanded.

"Nothing!" Imogen said quickly.

"Nothing at all," said Alex.

Amara felt Kalini tense. The last thing she needed was another argument, especially if they had a magical horse to help. She understood Alex and Imogen's concerns but she also trusted Ember.

"Hey, we're almost at the top," she said, trying to distract them all. "Look!" The ponies cantered up the last few metres of the hill. As they came out of the trees on to the ridgeway, Imogen, Alex, Amara and Kalini all gasped.

There, standing on the circle of bare earth and rock near the mountain spring, was a beautiful dapple-grey pony, rearing up, his outline silhouetted against the sky.

CHAPTER NINE

The pony's thick mane and tail swirled in the wind as he struck out at the air with his front legs. He was stunningly beautiful with dark grey dapples standing out on his snow-white coat and intelligent eyes that were wild and scared.

Alex's words burst out of him. "It's an elemental—"

"Alex!" Imogen cut across him. Amara saw her nod pointedly at Kalini. Luckily, Kalini didn't seem to have heard. She was staring at the pony, transfixed.

"Oh wow," she breathed.

We were right, Amara thought to Ember. *The wind wasn't anything to do with Ivy. It was this elemental horse.*

Scrambling off Ember, Kalini started heading towards the stallion.

"Kalini, be careful!" Amara called, feeling a lurch of anxiety. The pony looked like it was panicking and she was worried it would injure Kalini if she got too close. *Ember, we should stop her!*

Wait! he said, not moving.

Kalini's feet dislodged a stone. Hearing it skitter across the ground, the pony swung round to look at her. Amara's heart somersaulted. What would he do?

The wind dropped as the pony stared at Kalini and Kalini stared back. For a moment there was silence, as if the world was holding its breath.

And then with a wild whinny, the pony suddenly transformed! His coat darkened to a deep grey and he became stronger and more muscular. His mane and tail turned to white wisps and his eyes were an ebony black. He reared up, shaking his mane proudly.

"He's magic!" Kalini exclaimed, her eyes widening in shock as the stallion landed back on all four feet, his gaze on Kalini.

Kalini swung round to the others. Amara saw a frown darken her face as she realised they weren't as shocked as she was. "What's going on, guys?"

Amara didn't know what to say and from the look Alex and Imogen gave each other she was sure they felt the same.

Tell her about us, Amara, urged Ember.

I can't. We're not supposed to!

I think the horse and Kalini have a bond, Ember said quickly. *It's why she could hear him and the rest of you couldn't. Sometimes horses and their True Riders find each other like we did and sometimes they're drawn together like magnets. Tell her the truth!*

Kalini's frown deepened. "What's happening? Someone explain to me what's going on!"

Amara jumped off Ember and ran over to her best friend. "Kalini, there's something we need to tell you."

"Amara, no!" Imogen burst out, but Amara

ignored her. If Ember said it was OK then she believed him.

"There are magical horses in the world. They have powers over the elements. That grey horse is an elemental horse and it looks like he has power over storms." She watched Kalini's face as her friend took it all in. "Ember, Rose and Tide are elemental horses too," Amara rushed on. "All the games ponies at the stables are."

A look of understanding dawned. "So that's the big secret? I knew there was something you were all hiding!" Kalini said as Amara nodded.

"We couldn't tell you. True Riders are supposed to be the only ones who know the horses' secret."

"True Riders?" Kalini echoed.

"Each elemental horse chooses a person to be their one True Rider, to be their rider for life," Amara explained.

"Oh wow. So that's why you were so keen for me to ride Sparks yesterday?" said Kalini suddenly.

Amara nodded. "I'm sorry it didn't work out. And I'm sorry I've had to lie to you."

Kalini grabbed her in a hug. "It doesn't matter. I understand now."

"We can talk more later," said Amara, glancing at the horse, who was watching them. "What we need to do now is take the horse to Jill. She knows about elemental horses and she'll give him a home – if he wants it. Elemental horses don't belong to anyone, they choose who they want to be with and where they want to live."

"Rose and I will try and get him to come with us," said Alex. He rode Rose towards the stallion. But as they approached, the stallion reared up, his front legs striking out, his eyes flickering with fear again.

"It's OK," Alex called. "We just want to help you!" But the stallion was too panicked to listen. He stamped his front hooves into the churned-up ground and a blast of wind suddenly hurtled at Alex and Rose, knocking the chestnut pony to her knees.

"No! Don't hurt them!" cried Imogen, cantering Tide towards them.

The stallion sent another blast of wind, making Tide stumble too.

"It won't listen to us!" Alex shouted above the rain lashing down as the stallion panicked wildly.

Why is it doing this, Ember? Amara asked.

Sometimes horses don't realise they're elementals and then when they discover their powers it scares them.

"Let me try," said Kalini suddenly. Before they could stop her, she began walking towards the horse. He stopped rearing, the wind dying down again as the panic faded from his eyes. Kalini turned sideways and approached slowly, just as she had done with Bella in the field. "It's OK," she said softly. "I'm not going to hurt you. I . . ." She broke off, her eyes widening, and a moment later Amara saw her smile. Her lips moved slightly but no sound came out. The horse nodded.

"They're talking with their thoughts!" Amara exclaimed. She turned to Ember. "You were right! She does have a bond with him."

A true bond, he said, his eyes sparkling.

Kalini reached the horse. She put her hand out and, lowering his head, he let her stroke him. Then he lifted his muzzle to her face, his nostrils blowing in and out – the way all horses did when they wanted to make friends. Amara saw Kalini breathe gently back at him and place a hand on his neck.

"That's it, be calm now," she whispered.

But just then, hoofbeats shattered the silence. Ivy came galloping out of the trees on Bolt with Zara, Shannon and Daniela close behind her.

"Hands off!" Ivy snarled. "That horse is ours!"

CHAPTER TEN

An icy chill ran down Amara's spine as she saw that Ivy was holding a halter that was glowing an unearthly silver blue. Amara knew it was made of a binding rope that would burn any human apart from the person who had made it, and that it would force any horse wearing it to do Ivy's bidding. If Ivy got the halter on the stallion then he would have to go with her.

"Leave him alone!" Imogen exclaimed

furiously as Ivy left Zara, Shannon and Daniela by the trees and rode towards the stallion and Kalini.

"He's not yours to take!" shouted Alex. "He's an elemental horse. He should be allowed to choose where he goes."

Ivy laughed and twirled the halter. "He'll have to come with me when I get this on him."

Ember! We've got to stop her! urged Amara.

Leave it to me! With a fierce whinny, Ember transformed into his magical form. He grew taller, his eyes blazing with amber fire and his mane and tail changing to magical yellow and gold flames. Amara gasped as she felt the magic coursing through him, making her skin feel like it was glowing. "Go, Ember!" she shouted, grabbing his blazing mane as he leapt forward. He galloped in front of Ivy and Bolt, cutting between them and the stallion. Hearing the crackle of flames, Amara glanced back and saw Ember's hooves had left a trail of fire that now shot upwards, creating a flaming barrier between Ivy and the stallion. "You're brilliant, Ember!" she cried.

Ember wheeled round but Bolt had

transformed too, her eyes glowing red and her mane and tail prickling with lightning. Gathering herself, Bolt leapt over the flames.

"Girls, use your horses' powers!" ordered Ivy, her voice scalpel-sharp as Bolt landed near the stallion and Kalini. "Don't let them stop me!"

Shannon smirked. "Show them what you can do, Haze."

He banged his front hooves down and a

thick fog seeped from them, smothering the fire. He turned his glowing gaze to the Moonlight Stables horses and the dense fog swept straight at them, disorientating them.

As they urged their horses out of the smoke, they saw that Ivy was closing in on the stallion, the halter swinging from her hand.

"Stay away from him!" Kalini shouted. Grabbing a branch from the floor, she bravely ran towards Ivy and Bolt, but at the same moment the stallion whinnied fiercely and a huge fork of lightning hit the ground in front of Bolt, making her leap backwards. The halter flew from Ivy's hands as Bolt fell, trapping Ivy's leg beneath her.

"Get up, you stupid thing," Ivy shouted as Bolt clambered to her feet.

"Help!" gasped a voice. Amara turned to see Kalini rolling down towards the steep drop at the edge of the ridgeway. The lightning had knocked her over too.

"Kalini!" shrieked Amara in terror.

Just as Ember leapt forward to try and save her, a huge rhododendron bush sprouted up at the edge of the drop. Kalini crashed into its branches and came to a stop.

Amara almost burst into tears of relief. Turning, she saw that Rose had also transformed. Her mane and tail were now moss-green and covered with flowers, and her green eyes sparkled with silver light. Alex grinned and gave Amara a thumbs up.

"Are you OK, Kalini? Imogen called as Zara, Daniela and Shannon cantered over to help Ivy up.

Kalini's coat was torn and she had a scratch on her face but otherwise she was unhurt. "I'm fine," she said, scrambling to her feet.

Looking furious, Ivy tried to vault back on to Bolt but it was clear her leg was injured. She exclaimed with pain. "Capture that horse!" she hissed to Zara.

Zara urged Scorch towards where the magical halter lay on the ground. *She won't be able to pick it up; it'll burn her,* Amara thought, but then her heart sank as she realised that Zara was wearing thick gloves.

The stallion started to rear again, but before he could create another rumble of thunder, Quake made the ground under his hooves shake, unbalancing him and causing him to land back on all four feet. Haze then used his power to produce a thick black fog which surrounded the stallion, distracting him while Zara leant down from Scorch's back, reaching for the enchanted halter.

Amara felt the tingling of magic increase and knew that Ember was preparing to use his powers. "No, Ember, your magic's too dangerous. You can't use it on Zara!" she cried.

"But Tide can!" shouted Imogen. "Go, Tide!"

With a whinny, Tide transformed into her elemental form. She stamped her hooves and a little spring near the stallion suddenly exploded, the trickle turning into a torrent of water that shot straight at Zara and Scorch just as they reached the halter. Zara yelled as it knocked her off Scorch's back.

"Bullseye!" whooped Alex. He urged Rose

on and they galloped towards the halter. Leaning down from Rose's back, Alex grabbed the branch that Kalini had dropped earlier. He scooped the halter up on the end of it just like he'd practised for the litter-picking race, then wheeled Rose round and headed back towards Imogen and Amara, holding the stick aloft.

"Stop him!" Ivy screamed at Daniela and Shannon. They kicked their horses on.

Amara realised Alex was going to need help. "Come on, Ember!" she gasped.

Ember galloped to help protect Rose but Shannon and Daniela were closing in, Quake and Haze neck and neck. For one heart-stopping moment Amara thought they were going to snatch the halter from Alex but just as they drew close, Haze edged ahead of

Quake and Quake reacted angrily, biting his shoulder.

"Stop him doing that, Daniela!" shrieked Shannon.

"It's your fault, you shouldn't have let Haze get ahead!" shouted Daniela as Haze slowed down to bite Quake back.

"Amara! Take it!" Alex yelled, holding the stick out.

Amara felt a stab of panic. *What if she missed? What if she dropped it?*

You can do this, Amara! Ember encouraged her.

Amara focused all her attention on the stick. She heard Imogen's delighted yell as she reached over and grabbed it cleanly from Alex.

Ember raced to the edge of the steep drop

and skidded to a halt. Amara didn't think twice; she flung the stick and halter over the edge. They tumbled down into the steep ravine where no one could reach them. Ivy shrieked in dismay from up on Bolt's back.

"Look!" Zara yelled as she vaulted back on to Scorch. She pointed to the storm stallion.

He was rearing up, a whirlwind swirling around him as he prepared to conjure up a storm.

"Gallop!" Ivy yelled to Daniela, Zara and Shannon. Bolt raced away at lightning speed. Quake, Haze and Scorch followed, escaping into the trees and down the hill.

The stallion landed back on the ground, changing back into his pony form. The wind dropped and for a moment there was a stunned silence on the ridgeway.

"We did it," Amara breathed as all the ponies transformed back. "We fought them off."

"Way to go, us!" said Alex, but for once even he sounded shaky. "That was close."

"Very," said Imogen. "But we got rid of the halter and saved the horse." They all turned and looked at the stallion. Kalini was standing beside him, stroking his face.

"Now we just need to persuade him to come with us," said Alex.

Kalini gave them a smile. "I don't think that will be a problem. He says he'll come wherever I go." She stroked the stallion. "He's chosen me to be his True Rider."

Amara felt a bubbling swell of delight. "Oh, Kalini! That's amazing!"

"Totally! It'll be brilliant having you as a

True Rider too," said Imogen.

"And having you in the games squad," Alex added.

Kalini beamed.

"I wonder what Jill's going to say about it all?" said Amara.

There was the sound of a branch snapping behind them and they swung round to see Jill riding her horse, Apollo, out of the trees. She looked cross. "There you are! I saw the ponies had gone from the field and I've been searching high and low." Her eyes fell on Kalini and the stallion. "Will someone please tell me what's going on?"

Between them, Imogen, Amara, Alex and Kalini gabbled out everything that had happened. As she listened, Jill's face changed from cross to alarmed and finally to relieved.

"Well," she said, shaking her head when they finished. "I certainly didn't expect to hear any of that but it sounds like I should be very proud of you. Although next time please can you tell me before you go galloping off into a storm?"

"We will," they chorused sheepishly.

"I still don't really understand about elemental horses and True Riders," said Kalini.

Jill smiled at her. "I'll explain it all on the way home. The important thing is you are now a True Rider. The storm stallion has chosen you. What's his name?"

"Thunder," said Kalini.

Jill's smile grew wider. "In that case, welcome to Moonlight Stables, Kalini and Thunder!"

145

Amara's heart felt like it was going to beat out of her chest as the crowd around the mounted games arena roared. It was the final race of the competition and Moonlight Stables were beating Storm Stables by one point. Storm Stables were very fast but they had wasted time in a couple of earlier races by yelling at each other. Amara knew that if she could just take the stick cleanly and use it to pick the litter up then Moonlight Stables would win the race – and the competition!

Amara had felt much more confident after managing to grab the branch from Alex when it really mattered, and she had been practising handovers all week with Kalini.

The two of them had spent every evening in the meadow, splitting their time between passing a stick between them and helping Thunder learn how to control his magic. Now there was no need to keep the horses' magic secret from her best friend, Amara had found it much easier to concentrate and Jill had stopped talking about leaving her out of the competition.

I can do this, she thought determinedly.

Ember sidled impatiently as Alex and Rose turned at the top and began to gallop back down the arena towards them, Alex holding the stick out for Amara to take.

"Steady, Ember," Amara whispered. She could tell he was desperate to leap forward but she knew he mustn't go too soon.

Alex and Rose came hurtling towards

them. Daniela and Quake were neck and neck with them, while Zara waited to take their stick.

Amara released Ember's reins at just the right moment. He jumped forward and she grabbed the stick perfectly. *I've got it!* Amara thought, joy rushing through her.

"Go, Amara!" her teammates screamed.

Ember thundered up the arena and Amara used the stick to scoop the container up. She threw it cleanly into the bucket and they crossed the finish line. Amara punched the air and Ember bucked. They'd done it! They'd won the race for Moonlight Stables!

Looking back, she saw that Zara and Daniela had dropped the stick at the handover. Storm Stables had finished last and Zara was screaming furiously at Daniela.

"You didn't hand me the stick properly." Zara shouted at Daniela.

"It wasn't my fault!" Daniela yelled back. "You were the one who dropped it!"

Next to them, Alex, Imogen, Ollie and Jasmine were cheering, and Jill and Kalini were high-fiving.

Amara leant down and hugged Ember. *Thank you*, she told him as she rode over to her friends.

"Well done, Amara!" Jasmine yelled.

"You aced it!" exclaimed Ollie.

"You and Ember were brilliant," said Imogen, crowding round her with Alex and patting her on the back.

Kalini ran over. "Everyone was amazing," she said. "Moonlight Stables are the best!"

"We definitely deserve ice cream sundaes after this," said Alex.

"You are coming with us to Marco's, aren't you, Kalini?" Imogen asked.

Kalini smiled from ear to ear. "Absolutely!"

"And next weekend I vote we all have a sleepover at mine," said Alex.

"Ooh yes," said Imogen. "Alex has the best house for sleepovers," she told the others. "It's massive."

"We can have a training session, do some magic with the horses then go back to mine and have a midnight feast!" said Alex.

"It sounds amazing," said Kalini happily.

Looking at her friends' smiling faces, Amara didn't think she'd ever felt happier. Moonlight Stables had won the competition, but that wasn't what mattered most to her. The most important thing was that she and her friends were a team and Kalini and Thunder were now part of that team too.

Imogen and Alex left the ring with Kalini guiding Rose and Tide.

Amara and Ember followed them. *That was so much fun,* Ember said to Amara.

More fun than doing magic? she teased.

Ember stopped and turned to nuzzle her leg. *Nothing could be more fun than that!*

Amara stroked him. *I wonder what our next adventure will be? Do you think Ivy will try and cause trouble again?*

If she does, we'll stop her, Ember said. *She can't defeat the Moonlight Stables team!*

Alex looked round. "What are you two slowcoaches doing?"

"Yeah, hurry up," said Imogen. "In case you've forgotten, we've got a prize-giving to get ready for."

"And then ice creams to have!" said Kalini.

Rose and Tide whinnied as if calling them too.

Amara grinned. "OK, OK, we're coming!" She gathered up her reins and she and Ember walked across the bustling showground to catch up with their friends.

The End

Join the Moonlight Riders on
their next adventure in . . .
PETAL PONY
Read on for a sneak peek!

"There's a leak here! I need a bucket!" Amara
shouted.

Kalini came splashing through the
puddles, the hood of her pink coat pulled
up to protect her from the rain that was
cascading down from the grey sky. She thrust
a bucket over Ember's stable door. "Here you
go!"

"Thanks!" Amara said, grabbing it
gratefully and shoving it under the leak in
Ember's roof.

It had been raining heavily for the last few
days and when she and her friends, Kalini,
Alex and Imogen, had arrived at the yard
that morning they had found Jill Reed, the

owner of Moonlight Stables, trying to deal with leaks and overflowing water troughs.

Ember nuzzled Amara's plaits, water dripping from his coal-black forelock.

It's very wet in here! His mouth didn't move but Amara could hear his voice in her head. Ember, like the other eight beautiful ponies in the Meadow Stables block, was an elemental horse. Elemental horses were magic. They looked like regular ponies most of the time but they could transform into their true shape whenever they wanted to and they each had their own special powers. Ember was a fire horse who could make things burst into flame.

To be continued . . .

True Rider: Amara Thompson

Age:
10

Appearance:
Brown hair and blue eyes

Lives with:
Parents

Best friend:
Kalini

Favourite things to do:
Anything with horses, drawing and reading pony stories

Favourite mounted game:
Bending race

I most want to improve:
Vaulting on and off at speed and getting my handovers right

Elemental Horse: Ember

Colour:
Black

Height:
14.1hh

Personality:
Loving, lively, hot-tempered

Pony breed:
Welsh section B x
Thoroughbred

Elemental appearance:
Golden eyes, swirling mane and a magical, fiery tail

Elemental abilities:
Fire Horse - Ember can create fires, make things burst into flame and cast fire balls from his hooves

True Rider: Imogen Fairfax

Age:
10

Appearance:
Light brown hair and hazel eyes

Lives with:
Mum, Dad, two brothers Will (17) and Tim (15), Minnie our cockapoo

Best friend:
Alex

Favourite things to do:
Anything with horses, walking Minnie, helping at my gran's teashop

Favourite mounted game:
Mug shuffle

I most want to improve:
My accuracy in races

Elemental Horse: Tide

Colour:
White-grey

Height:
14.1hh

Personality:
Thoughtful, sensitive and kind

Pony breed:
Arab x Welsh

Elemental appearance:
Blue eyes, silver-blue coat and a flowing sea foam mane and tail

Elemental abilities:
Water Horse - Tide can make it rain and manipulate bodies of water to create waves, whirlpools and waterspouts

True Rider: Alex Brahler

Age:
11

Appearance:
Black hair and dark brown eyes

Lives with:
Mum, Dad, sister Frankie
(15) and our chocolate Labradors,
Scooby and Murphy

Best friend:
Imogen

Favourite things to do:
Anything with horses, playing
football, cross-country running,
climbing and swimming

Favourite mounted game:
Five-flag race

I most want to improve:
Being more patient in
competitions so I'm not
eliminated by starting races
before the flag falls!

Elemental Horse: Rose

Colour:
Bright chestnut with flaxen
mane and tail, a white blaze
and four white socks

Height:
14.2 hh

Personality:
Patient, calm, confident

Pony Breed:
Welsh section C

Elemental appearance:
Bright green eyes, a mossy green
mane and tail covered in flowers

Elemental abilities:
Earth Horse - Rose can make plants
and flowers grow

Night Rider: Zara Watson

Age:
11

Appearance:
Blonde hair and green eyes

Lives with:
Mum most of the time
and Dad some of the time

Best friend:
Daniella (my cousin)

Favourite things to do:
Riding, playing tennis, shopping,
pamper sessions

Favourite mounted game:
Bottle race

I most want to improve:
Nothing, I'm good at everything

Elemental Horse: Scorch

Colour:
Bright chestnut with a white blaze

Height:
14.2hh

Personality:
Lively, mean, impatient

Pony Breed:
Show Pony x Thoroughbred

Elemental appearance:
Red eyes, mane and tail of dark
flickering flames

Elemental abilities:
Fire Horse - although not as
powerful as Ember, Scorch can heat
things up and cause small fires

Moonlight Riders

Meet all the True Riders of Moonlight
Stables and their amazing elemental horses!

Moonlight Riders

Petal Pony

LINDA CHAPMAN

Do you have what it takes to become a True Rider?